BUTTERFLIES

by Michèle Dufresne

Pioneer Valley Educational Press, Inc.

A butterfly is an insect.

A butterfly has six legs
and four wings.

A butterfly has a small body.

There are three parts
to a butterfly's body: the head,
the middle part called the **thorax**,
and the back part called the **abdomen**.

head

thorax

abdomen

5

A butterfly has two **antennae**.
Butterflies use their antennae to smell.

A butterfly has a mouth
that is really a long tube.
Butterflies use their long tube
like a drinking straw.

A mother butterfly lays her eggs
on plants. She chooses plants
that her babies can use as food.

Most butterfly eggs hatch in a few days or weeks.

A **caterpillar** comes out of the egg.

The caterpillar eats and eats.
It grows and grows. It grows
until it is too big for its skin.
The skin pops open, and the caterpillar
crawls out with a new skin.
It starts eating and growing again.

When the caterpillar is done growing, it hooks its body to a leaf or branch. Then the caterpillar's skin comes off for the last time. Under the old skin is a new, hard skin called a **chrysalis**.

Inside the chrysalis, the caterpillar
is changing into a butterfly.
When the caterpillar is ready,
the chrysalis splits open.

The caterpillar has turned
into a butterfly!
This is called **metamorphosis**.

GLOSSARY

abdomen: the rear part of an insect's body

antennae: a pair of long sense organs on the head of an insect

caterpillar: the worm-like stage of a butterfly

chrysalis: the hard covering that protects a butterfly as it forms from a caterpillar

metamorphosis: a series of changes in the life cycle of an insect

thorax: the middle part of an insect's body